W9-DEW-603

DISCARD

DISCARD

PROPERTY OF C L P L

SPOTLIGHT ON CIVIC ACTION

CIVIC ROLES IN THE COMMUNITY
HOW CITIZENS GET INVOLVED

CASSANDRA RICHARDS

PowerKiDS press™

NEW YORK

Published in 2018 by The Rosen Publishing Group, Inc.
29 East 21st Street, New York, NY 10010

Copyright © 2018 by The Rosen Publishing Group, Inc.

All rights reserved. No part of this book may be reproduced in any form without permission in writing from the publisher, except by a reviewer.

Editor: Theresa Morlock
Book Design: Michael Flynn
Interior Layout: Tanya Dellaccio

Photo Credits: Cover Fuse/Corbis/Getty Images; p. 5 Winston Tan/Shutterstock.com; p. 6 Diego Grandi/
Shutterstock.com; p. 7 https://commons.wikimedia.org/wiki/File:Susanna_Madora_Salter.jpg;
p. 8 Blend Images - Hill Street Studios/Brand X Pictures/Getty Images; p. 9 Courtesy of the Library of Congress;
p. 11 Pacific Press/LightRocket/Getty Images; p. 13 Chip Somodevilla/Getty Images News/Getty Images;
p. 14 Chris Graythen/Getty Images News/Getty Images; p. 15 https://commons.wikimedia.org/wiki/
File:Clara_Barton_1904.jpg; p. 17 asiseeit/E+/Getty Images; p. 18 Bloomberg/Getty Images; pp. 19, 21 kali9/E+/
Getty Images; p. 20 Steve Hamann/Shutterstock.com; p. 23 Inmagineasia/Getty Images; p. 25 https://
commons.wikimedia.org/wiki/File:Rosaparks.jpg; p. 26 AFP/Getty Images; p. 27 a katz/Shutterstock.com;
p. 29 Michael Kovac/WireImage/Getty Images.

Cataloging-in-Publication Data

Names: Richards, Cassandra.
Title: Civic roles in the community: how citizens get involved / Cassandra Richards.
Description: New York : PowerKids Press, 2018. | Series: Spotlight on civic action | Includes index.
Identifiers: ISBN 9781538327883 (pbk.) | ISBN 9781508164043 (library bound) | ISBN 9781538328002 (6 pack)
Subjects: LCSH: Social action--Juvenile literature. | Youth--Political activity--Juvenile literature. | Social advocacy--
Juvenile literature. | Political participation--Juvenile literature. | Voluntarism--Juvenile literature.
Classification: LCC HQ784.V64 R53 2018 | DDC 362.0425--dc23

Manufactured in China

CPSIA Compliance Information: Batch #BW18PK For further information contact Rosen Publishing, New York, New York at 1-800-237-9932.

CONTENTS

CHAPTER ONE

PRIVILEGES AND DUTIES

There are many wonderful privileges that come with being a U.S. citizen. You probably experience many of these privileges in your daily life and may even take them for granted. Citizens in a community have access to schools, libraries, and parks. They have police and fire departments to call when they're in trouble. They have street cleaning and garbage-collection services to take care of their needs. Being part of a community that offers helpful services improves your life as a citizen. It's your duty as a citizen to contribute to the community you live in.

A local government of elected officials makes and maintains policies about how the community operates and manages the community's services and institutions. By being an involved citizen, you can help make decisions about how your community works.

Citizens contribute to their communities by paying taxes. The government uses the money from taxes to pay for city parks and other community services and institutions.

CHAPTER TWO

BEING AWARE

Learning about how your community works is the first step in becoming an active citizen. Just as there are federal and state governments, there are local governments to manage the communities in which we live. It's important to understand the structure of your local government.

There are two main kinds of local government: **county** and **municipality**. Counties may also be called

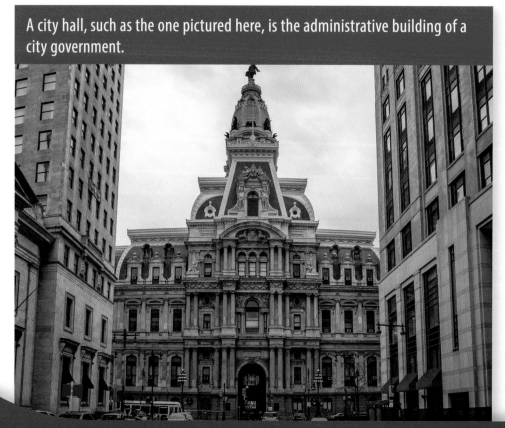

A city hall, such as the one pictured here, is the administrative building of a city government.

The mayor is the highest-ranking official in some kinds of municipal government. Susanna Madora Salter—who became mayor of Argonia, Kansas, in 1887—was the first female mayor in the United States.

boroughs in certain places. These forms of local government are structured differently and offer different kinds of services to their communities.

Who's in charge of your local government? This can vary depending on where you live. In some county governments, voters elect a board of **commissioners** and a county executive. In some municipal governments, voters elect a mayor, a council, and a board of commissioners. These elected officials make important decisions for the community.

CHAPTER THREE

SPEAK WITH YOUR VOTE

Voters decide who's elected to the local government. By voting, you can take an active role in shaping the future of your community. Although many people participate in the presidential election, it's even more important to vote in local elections because fewer votes may decide the election.

This is a picture of voting booths. Voting booths make sure that each citizen's vote is private.

People who supported women's suffrage were called suffragists. This photo shows a suffragist parade in New York City in 1912.

The right to vote is called suffrage. Throughout American history, the right to vote has marked the level of freedom of American citizens. African American men weren't granted the right to vote until 1870, when the 15th Amendment was ratified. American women were denied the right to vote until the 19th Amendment was ratified in 1920. Without the right to vote, people have no say in who runs the government. Exercising your right to vote is one of the most important ways you can get involved in your community.

CHAPTER FOUR

VOICE YOUR OPINIONS

Another way to voice your opinions is to attend public meetings. Town hall meetings are events at which people discuss community issues. Local politicians attend these meetings to answer questions from citizens. Boards of education also hold meetings that are open to the public. This kind of board makes decisions about local public schools. You can find out how the schools are being run and voice your opinions about it.

Another way to share your thoughts and concerns is to write a letter to the editor of your local newspaper. Letters to the editor are published in every newspaper edition. You can also speak out on some local websites, but be sure to ask your parents for help.

When attending a public meeting it's very important to be polite. Listen carefully and be sure you understand the rules for making a statement.

CHAPTER FIVE

JOIN A GROUP

You can get involved in your community by joining a group that shares your interests. Many municipalities have a historical society that aims to preserve historic places and **artifacts** and educate the public about local history. If you're interested in wildlife conservation or animal rescue, you could join an **advocacy** group that does outdoor cleanup projects or fundraising **campaigns** for those causes.

Some groups have been created especially for young people. The Girl Scouts and Boy Scouts of America are leadership programs in which kids can learn about responsibility and contributing to the community. Another community program that teaches young people about active citizenship through hands-on projects is 4-H. These organizations offer kids and teens opportunities to learn about their communities and take part in improving them.

Programs such as the Girl Scouts of America encourage members to volunteer to take an active part in making their communities a better place. This photo shows First Lady Michelle Obama hosting a camp-out for Girl Scouts on the White House lawn in 2015.

CHAPTER SIX

NONPROFIT ORGANIZATIONS

Nonprofit organizations are groups dedicated to a particular mission or cause. Some examples of nonprofit organizations include the American Red Cross, Goodwill Industries, and Habitat for Humanity. These organizations work to effect change on local, national, and international levels. Branches of these nonprofits and similar organizations can be found in communities around the country.

These Habitat for Humanity volunteers are building a home in Violet, Louisiana.

Clara Barton founded the American Red Cross in 1881.

The American Red Cross offers many services, including providing emergency relief and accepting and distributing blood donations. By giving blood to the Red Cross or similar organizations, you could help save someone's life. Goodwill Industries helps boost communities by employing veterans and people who face challenges finding jobs. Habitat for Humanity builds affordable houses for people with low incomes in struggling communities. You can make a difference in your community by donating money to a nonprofit, educating people about what they do, or volunteering with them.

CHAPTER SEVEN

VOLUNTEER

One of the best ways for any person to take an active role in their community is to volunteer. Volunteering means giving your time and energy to help out without expecting anything in return. It's good for the community and for you. Volunteering can help you learn new skills, meet new people, and take pride in yourself. There are many ways for people to volunteer.

Volunteers are often needed at soup kitchens and nursing homes. A soup kitchen is a place where people who are homeless or need help can come to eat meals. You might be able to help set tables, cook, pass out food, wash dishes, or even simply talk to people while they eat. You could visit a nursing home to read to elderly people or spend time playing games with them.

Running a food drive is another way to help people in need. You could ask members of your community to give canned goods to feed the hungry.

CHAPTER EIGHT

BECOME A PUBLIC SERVANT

Civic participation can take many forms. It could mean voting, raising awareness about an issue, getting involved in a group, or volunteering. Some people take an active role in their community by choosing a career that allows them to manage the way the community is run or help the people within the community. These people are called public servants.

Some public service jobs require applicants to take a civil service exam. This is a test that determines if a person is suited to a particular job.

Some public service jobs focus on providing people with access to the basic things they need to survive, such as clean water, electricity, gas, and waste management. Other public servants provide medical care and help during emergencies such as fires. Public transportation and libraries are also types of public services, as are the postal service and public broadcasting. The main types of public service jobs are public health and safety, public **administration**, and education.

Public administrators manage governments. Some types of public administrators are city managers, treasurers, and mayors. These people manage public programs and enforce government policies.

Public health and safety workers help protect community members from harmful situations. Local health and safety workers could include police officers, firefighters, doctors, nurses, and other medical professionals. Public servants may also work for agencies that test food products to make sure they're safe for people to consume.

Sanitation workers are public servants, too.

Public school teachers and administrators are public servants because they educate the youth of America. These workers are dedicated to producing responsible, informed citizens who will contribute to their communities and their country. Crossing guards and bus drivers can also be thought of as public servants. These workers are committed to getting children to school and back home safely.

CHAPTER NINE

CONTACT LOCAL OFFICIALS

Even if you're too young to have a job in public service, you can be actively involved in your community by communicating with your local public servants. You can call, e-mail, or write a letter to your local officials to let them know how you feel about their actions and policies. Most local governments have a website on which contact information for local officials can be found. If you're happy with their service or policies, you can let them know that you're grateful for their hard work.

Organizing or taking part in a letter-writing campaign is a useful way to communicate with government officials. You can write to local government administrators or even to the president of the United States! Your letter could include information about yourself, an issue of concern, and your suggested solution to that issue.

Letter-writing campaigns are often used to let elected officials know what issues citizens are concerned about.

CHAPTER TEN

DIRECT ACTION

Direct action means using strikes, demonstrations, and protests to effect change in the community. Nonviolent direct action was a major part of the civil rights movement of the 1950s and 1960s. Civil rights **activists** staged **sit-ins**, **boycotts**, and nonviolent acts of resistance to draw attention to problems in the community and offer possible solutions.

More recently, citizens used direct action to protest North Carolina's House Bill 2, more commonly called the bathroom bill. This piece of legislation required people, including **transgender** people, to only use public bathrooms for the gender assigned to them at birth. In response to the bill, many people in North Carolina and elsewhere protested by boycotting facilities with **discriminatory** bathroom rules. The bill was eventually replaced. You can be an active citizen by figuring out ways to protest or work against policies you disagree with.

Rosa Parks sparked the Montgomery bus boycott by refusing to give up her seat to a white man. This boycott led to the end of discriminatory bus laws in Montgomery.

CHAPTER ELEVEN

DEMONSTRATIONS AND PROTESTS

Public demonstrations and protests are ways to send messages to the government about how you feel about its policies. Some of the greatest progress for human rights in America has been achieved with the help of public demonstrations. The March on Washington, which took place in 1963, is one of the most famous demonstrations

MARTIN LUTHER KING JR.

On November 13, 2016, 3,000 protesters marched in New York City to express their opposition to Donald Trump's proposed immigration policies.

in American history. More than 200,000 people gathered in Washington, D.C., to show their support for equal rights for African Americans and listen to Martin Luther King Jr. give his famous "I Have a Dream" speech.

Some recent movements that have organized demonstrations include the Occupy Wall Street, Black Lives Matter, LGBTQ, and women's movements. By participating in a demonstration, you can voice your opinion about government policies or conditions in your community.

CHAPTER TWELVE

SOCIAL ENTREPRENEURSHIP

If you feel that your community is missing something important, you can start a project to fill that need. A social entrepreneur is someone who creates an **enterprise** to solve a problem or bring about a change in the community. Social entrepreneurs use their talents, energy, and leadership abilities to create businesses or ventures to improve the lives of others.

You don't need to own a business to be a social entrepreneur. You could start a community garden to bring healthy, fresh food to the people of your city or town. You could ask people to donate extra books to make your own lending library. You could clean up litter or ask permission to plant trees or flowers. You could do something as simple as having a lemonade stand to raise money for a cause you believe in.

TOMS and

One for One

Some social entrepreneurs own companies. Blake Mycoskie is the founder of TOMS, a shoe company that donates a pair of shoes to charity every time a customer buys a pair.

CHAPTER THIRTEEN

GET INVOLVED

The citizens who make up a community are responsible for making it a positive and productive place to live. By being an involved citizen, you can address your needs and the needs of others within your community. You can be a force for social change by learning about how your community works, voicing your opinion, volunteering, and participating in direct action.

Think about all the ways you experience the privileges of citizenship. You might get where you need to go using public transportation, such as a subway or bus. You may attend a public school, which provides opportunities to improve your life and future through education. You can contact police officers, firefighters, and medical professionals if you're in trouble. How can you take a more active role as a citizen within your community?

GLOSSARY

activist (AK-tih-vist) Someone who acts strongly in support of or against an issue.

administration (uhd-mih-nuh-STRAY-shun) The activities that relate to running a government, company, school, or other organization.

advocacy (ADD-voh-kuh-see) The act of supporting a cause or policy.

artifact (AR-tih-fakt) Something made by humans in the past that still exists.

boycott (BOY-kaht) A refusal to buy, use, or participate in something.

campaign (kam-PAYN) A plan to achieve a certain result.

commissioner (kuh-MIH-shuh-nur) Someone who is elected to be responsible for administering the government.

county (COWN-tee) An area within a state that provides local government services.

discriminatory (dis-KRIH-muh-nuh-toh-ree) Treating a person or group of people badly or unfairly because they are different.

enterprise (EN-tuhr-pryz) A project or undertaking.

municipality (myoo-nih-sih-PAL-uh-tee) A city or town with its own government.

sit-in (SIT–in) A protest in which people sit or stay in a place and refuse to leave.

transgender (tranz-JEN-duhr) A person whose gender identity is different from the anatomy they were born with.

INDEX

PRIMARY SOURCE LIST

Page 7
Susanna M. Salter. Photograph. ca. 1887. Now kept at the Kansas Historical Society.

Page 9
Youngest parader in New York City suffragist parade. Photograph by the American Press Association. May 4, 1912. Now kept at the Library of Congress Prints and Photographs Division, Washington, D.C.

Page 15
Clara Barton ca. 1890. Photograph. Now kept at the Library of Congress Prints and Photographs Division, Washington, D.C.

WEBSITES

Due to the changing nature of Internet links, PowerKids Press has developed an online list of websites related to the subject of this book. This site is updated regularly. Please use this link to access the list: www.powerkidslinks.com/sociv/roles